GOLF

THE ESSENTIAL GUIDE FOR YOUNG GOLFERS

CLIVE GIFFORD

KINGFISHER
NEW YORK

Contents

The glorious game

Golf is an exciting sport of power, accuracy, and nerve that offers a constant challenge to players. You use a club to hit a ball into a small hole or cup in as few shots as possible. A regular round of golf involves playing 18 different holes on a course. Each hole will test you and your skills in different ways. Millions of people play golf for fun, while at the highest level, top professional golfers earn fortunes playing in competitions. At all levels, golf is a game you can play throughout your life. Lorens Chan was just 14 when he played in the 2009 Sony Open, while Jerry Barber was 77 when he played in a professional tournament in 1994.

Golfers tend to dress up for the course. They usually wear nice pants or skirts and short-sleeved, collared shirts that fit loose enough to allow their arms and body to move freely. A sweater is worn in colder weather, and waterproof pants and jackets are also packed for wet weather play.

There are more than 20,000 golf courses around the world. At about 10,960 ft. (3,340m) above sea level, the La Paz golf club in Bolivia is the highest 18-hole golf course in the world.

A golf club is swung back and then down and forward in a large circular motion to hit the ball at the bottom of the downswing. The winding and unwinding of a golfer's body and arms can generate great power—top players can hit a ball well over 330 yd. (300m).

"Golf is deceptively simple and endlessly complicated."

Arnold Palmer

Tiger Woods has been the leading golfer for more than a decade and scored his first hole in one at the age of six! He is pictured here at 14 years old, already a formidable talent.

While many shots are hit long distances, success often comes down to short shots on the green, called putts, to send the ball into the hole.

HOLE IN ONE: hitting the ball straight into the hole from the tee

Golf terms

In the bag

A set of golf clubs consists of a number of woods, irons, wedges, and an almost flat-faced putter for use on the green. Smaller, younger players can use shorter, junior-length clubs, which are easier to handle and swing. Beginners also tend to start playing with a half set of clubs with two woods, three or four irons, a wedge, and a putter.

Driver, or 1-wood

A golfer's bag is used to store spare balls and items such as waterproof clothing, an umbrella, and a bottle of water. A golfer is allowed up to 14 clubs in their bag, from the driver, or 1-wood, which is the longest club in the bag, to wedges, which are the most "lofted" clubs in the bag and are used for short, high shots.

3-iron

Putter

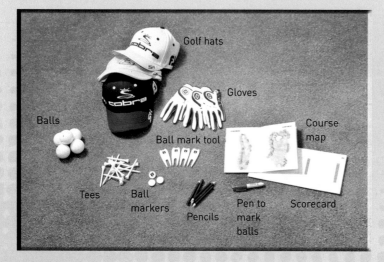

Golf hats

Gloves

Balls

Ball mark tool

Course map

Tees

Ball markers

Pencils

Pen to mark balls

Scorecard

Above are some of the other items that golfers carry in their bags. Tees raise a ball off the ground. Ball mark repair tools are used to raise and repair ground dented by the ball's landing.

Wood covers protect clubheads

Golf clubs have different amounts of loft on their clubface, as shown above. The 3-iron (front) will send the ball lower and longer than the 9-iron (back).

6-iron

9-iron

Bottom of clubhead is called the sole

Sand wedge

A golf glove is worn on your left hand if you play right-handed. It should fit tightly and helps improve your grip and prevent blisters.

Woods have a large clubhead and are used to hit the ball long distances. Irons are numbered up to nine. Lower-numbered clubs send the ball much lower in the air but over longer distances. The higher the number, the more angle, or loft, there is on the clubface and the higher the ball travels in flight.

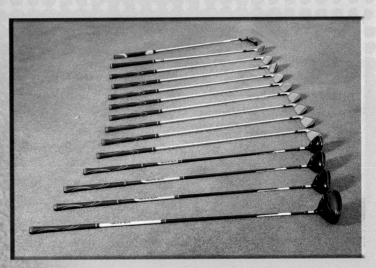

A golf club consists of a long shaft with a rubber or leather grip at one end and the clubhead at the other. The broad, flat part that strikes the ball is called the clubface.

LOFT: the amount of angle on the clubface

Golf terms

The golf course

A full round of golf lasts 18 holes. Holes measure different lengths and pose different challenges. Each starts with a teeing area and ends with a smooth green in which a 4.25-in. (10.8-cm)-wide hole is marked by a flagpole. In between the tee and the green can lie trees, long grass called rough, bunkers filled with sand, and ponds and streams known as water hazards.

Always check out the course map or diagram, which is often found at the course clubhouse or on the back of a scorecard. It will give you an idea of the challenges you face.

Dogleg

Water hazard

Sensible thinking and careful planning are the keys to getting around the course with a good score.

Bunker

Rough

Greenskeepers, here riding lawnmowers, ensure that a golf course is kept in immaculate condition. You can also help by not leaving litter and by repairing any damage that you may do to the ground, such as divots (see page 31).

When on a golf course, always play quickly so you do not delay other golfers behind you.

Many golf courses have practice areas where golfers can warm up before a round. These young golfers are working on their putting on the practice putting green.

A hole that has a kink or angle in its fairway so that you cannot see the green from the tee is called a dogleg. Players may have to play a shorter or shaped shot in order to get the ball around the corner.

Fairway

Trees

Tee

Green

Each hole starts with a teeing area from where the ball is driven. Pairs of colored markers show the teeing positions for juniors and women, men, and competitions.

TEEING AREA: the marked-out area at the start of a hole

Golf terms

Playing a hole

Golfers play a course in groups of up to four players. A golfer's first shot is a drive from the teeing area. Their last shot on a hole will be the shot that sends the ball into the cup, or hole, on the green. From the start to the finish, all golfers must follow the rules of the sport and act politely and considerately (this is called etiquette). This includes staying quiet and still whenever another golfer is playing a shot.

A round usually starts on the first hole, although golfers may be directed by course signs to begin on a different hole. Wherever you start, try to play with as few delays as possible. If you are holding up other golfers, you should wave them through so that they can play the hole and move on ahead of you.

This player has completed her second shot from the fairway. Play a shot only when golfers ahead of you are well out of your maximum range.

You start a hole by teeing up your ball and driving. Other players stand far away, stay silent, and watch where the ball travels so that they can direct the golfer if she fails to spot it in the air.

These players walk off the green briskly after completing the hole. Always treat greens carefully—repair any ball marks, leave your bag off the green, replace the flag after completing the hole, and never run.

This golfer has been asked to attend the flag, holding it upright and then pulling it out of the ball's way. If your putt hits the flagstick, you add two penalty shots to your score.

Once on the green, a golfer uses their putter to putt the ball. They can remove loose items on the green such as leaves before they putt if they wish to.

Scoring terms per hole	
Eagle	2 shots under par
Birdie	1 shot under par
Par	
Bogey	1 shot over par
Double bogey	2 shots over par

Keep an honest count of the shots that you take, including any accidental nudges of the ball or air shots where you completely miss the ball. If you hit a shot badly and fear that it might travel near other golfers, immediately shout "fore!" as a warning. If you hear that shout from someone else, put your arms over your head and duck down for protection.

A course's scorecard lists each hole's par score. This is the number of shots a very good player is expected to take to complete a hole. Always mark your score after leaving a green.

Masterclass

This player's ball has ended up in the rough to the right of the fairway. He uses a short iron with a lot of loft to get the ball up and out of trouble.

This golfer plays a short chip shot, aiming for the green. When playing in a group, the golfer with the shot farthest from the hole plays first.

Greg Norman
Australia's greatest professional golfer, Greg Norman was known for his long, accurate drives that often put him in a great position to reach the green and get a birdie.

Golf terms **BALL MARKS:** dents in the green caused by a golf ball's landing

Starting out

A full golf course can feel like an intimidating place when you've just started to play. Fortunately, there are many other places where you can practice your shots and build your golf game, from open fields and putting greens to pitch-and-putt courses and driving ranges. Pitch-and-putts are scaled-down golf courses with 30–100-yd. (30–100-m) holes found in many parks and resorts. They can offer an excellent test of your shorter shots and putting.

You can practice short-pitch and chip shots using a target such as one or more upturned umbrellas to aim the ball into.

At a driving range, you buy a bucket or basket of balls that you hit from a designated hitting station. Most driving ranges have distance markers and flags. Watch where your ball lands and rolls. Over time, you will get a better idea of how far you can hit the ball with each club in your bag.

Situated in the center of Tokyo, Japan, Jingu Driving Range has 163 hitting stations on three different floors. At a driving range you can practice your shots without having to walk to collect the ball.

For many children, their first golfing experience is playing miniature golf. They putt the ball around, over, or through a series of obstacles and into the hole.

Putting greens are found in some parks. If it's not busy, practice hitting three or four balls at each hole, adjusting your aim and strength of putt based on your previous shots.

Masterclass

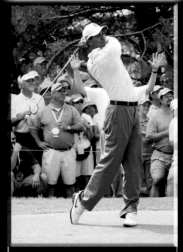

TIGER WOODS
Top players such as Tiger Woods never hit balls on a driving range aimlessly. Instead, they take their time and think through each shot. They vary their practice sessions to keep them interesting and might start with some short shots to build rhythm.

PUTT : shot using a putter where the ball rolls along the ground

Golf terms

Grip it!

A good golf swing starts with an accurate, controlled grip of the club. A good grip helps the clubface meet the ball squarely and accurately. The club is gripped in front of you. Start by letting your arms and hands hang down naturally and then grip the club with your left hand if you are a right-handed golfer. (Grip with your right if you are left-handed.) Your other hand wraps around and ensures that the club is balanced and under control.

The grip will feel strange at first, but practice gripping a club as often as possible and it will start to feel natural. Try to hold the club relatively lightly in your fingers and not in your palm. Think "hold" rather than "grip."

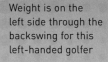

Weight is on the left side through the backswing for this left-handed golfer

Keep your weight on the inside of your back foot and don't let your weight move too far away from the center.

Before gripping and swinging, it's a good idea to stretch your body's muscles for the vigorous effort ahead. Stretching also helps prevent injuries.

Bring your arm across your body, level with the ground. Hold the stretch for ten seconds.

Hold a club at either end and swivel your hips to turn and stretch your back and sides.

To perform this wrist stretch, grasp your fingers and pull them back toward your body.

Rest the grip between your lower palm and where your fingers join the palm of your left hand.

Bring your hand around so that the club rests in the last three fingers of your hand. Your thumb should point down the grip, slightly to the right of center.

The Vardon grip (also known as the overlapping grip) sees the little finger of the top hand rest on the groove between the first and middle fingers of the bottom hand.

Right thumb points down the club, left of center

Masterclass

Harry Vardon
There are different types of grips used to hold a club. Great Britain's Harry Vardon popularized the overlapping grip so that it became known as the Vardon grip. Vardon was one of golf's first superstars, winning the 1900 U.S. Open and six British Opens.

The interlocking grip sees the little finger of the right hand interlock with the first finger of the left hand.

The baseball grip sees the hands placed side by side with no overlapping or interlocking.

BACKSWING: the movement of the club back and away from the ball

Golf terms

Lining it up

With your club gripped, now is the time to line up your shot. Getting the club behind the ball with the clubface pointing toward the target, and your body in the right place for your swing, is known as the set-up, or address, position. Try to get into the habit of using the same routine each time you get into the address position. This will help you produce accurate shots.

The distance of your feet from the ball varies depending on your club. Woods and longer irons see you stand farther away from the ball. Shorter clubs like a 9-iron will see you stand closer.

Always take time to set up carefully. Although golf shots are played over long distances, being out of line by a couple of inches can lead to your shot landing many yards wide of your target.

Club rests gently on, or hovers just above, the ground

Shoulders line up parallel to club's line

Bend forward from the hips

Back straight

Head looking down but with chin up

Right shoulder a little lower because right hand grips lower than left

Knees slightly flexed

To set up your address position, you start by lining up your clubface squarely behind the ball so that it points to your target.

Placing both hands on the club to grip it correctly, the golfer steps into the address position, getting their feet pointing in a line parallel to the direction that the club is pointing.

Your arms hang down from your shoulders. This helps generate a space between your legs and your hands gripping the club.

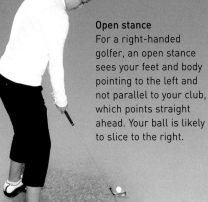

Open stance
For a right-handed golfer, an open stance sees your feet and body pointing to the left and not parallel to your club, which points straight ahead. Your ball is likely to slice to the right.

Closed stance
A closed stance has your feet pointing too far to the right. It often occurs when a golfer points their feet at the target. The ball is likely to hook left of target.

Sitting and sagging
A common mistake is to let your bottom drop down into a "sitting on a stool" position. This makes it difficult to swing well.

Body angled forward from waist

Weight is evenly over both feet

Viewed from above, your feet, hips, and shoulders should point along a line parallel to the line that you want to hit the ball along.

Masterclass

Ernie Els
South African Ernie Els is known as the "Big Easy" for his graceful, smooth golf swing. Els ensures that he is perfectly lined up at the address position so that his powerful swing sends the ball a long distance but exactly on target.

Line formed by feet runs parallel to target

Club placed along toes to show where feet are pointing

Ball's direction to target

Aim your club, not your body, at the target.

SLICE: a shot that spins or curves away far to the right of the target for a right-handed player

Head stays
focused on
the ball

Body weight
is over the
right foot

1 After taking several
gentle practice
swings, start in the
address position
with your feet, body,
and club well lined
up with the target.

2 Turning your shoulders,
begin the backswing by
taking the club away
from the ball. Keep the
clubhead low and your
wrists straight until the
club passes the horizontal.

3 Your wrists hinge or
cock as your shoulde
continue turning and
club travels back and
behind your head. You
left shoulder travels
under your head, whi
stays focused on the

Knees
slightly
bent and
body well
balanced

Clubface
pointing
to target

Hit it!

While a full golf swing is broken down into different
parts for teaching, it is actually one continuous,
smooth movement. Once aligned well at the
address position, you take the club back, low at
first, turning from your shoulders, with the rest of
your body and arms following. As the backswing
continues, your wrists bend or hinge as the club
sweeps up and behind your head to complete the
backswing. At the top of the backswing, your body
is wound up like a spring. The unwinding as the
club swings down is what gives a full swing its
power. This should be natural, unhurried, and
unforced. Don't push the club down with your right
hand. Instead, pull your left hand and arm down
toward the ball as your body starts to turn back.

Body weight shifts from right foot to left

Right leg bends at the knee

Left leg is straight

4 Leading from the shoulders first, start to unwind your body, turning as your left arm pulls the club down and toward the ball.

5 Your wrists unhinge, and the clubhead lags behind your hands through the downswing until the ball is struck. Your head should stay down and still.

6 The club sweeps briskly through the ball, sending it flying away. Look to make clean, crisp contact, with the middle of the clubface striking the whole of the ball.

7 The hips continue to turn as the club follows through high and over your shoulder. You should end with your belt buckle pointing directly toward the target.

As your body turns on the downswing, your weight moves from over your right foot to over your left. After the clubface strikes the ball, your body continues turning as the club travels on its long follow-through. Keep your head pointing down until your right shoulder comes through under your chin. Complete your swing with a well-balanced finish, with your chest facing the target and your weight balanced over your left leg with the right foot turned and lifted. Remember, the key to a long, accurate shot is not brute force but keeping a smooth, unhurried rhythm.

Masterclass

Lorena Ochoa
Former world number one Lorena Ochoa is small in stature yet often hits the ball farther and more accurately than her rivals. Her secret is a swing, well-grooved in practice, that has perfect timing to generate power.

Maintain your grip as you swing, but not too tightly. You want control, but without tensing up your hands and arms.

Make sure you keep the club hovering just above the ground on the first inch or so of the takeaway from the ball.

Keep your head down and still and your eyes on the ball throughout the shot. Your head moves only as you follow through, swiveling around.

TAKEAWAY: the first part of the backswing where the club travels low over the ground away from the ball

Golf terms

Head stays down—focus on where the ball would be

Shoulder turn

Weight on right side during backswing

The body and arm movements of a swing can be practiced anywhere —even without a club. Think about the different movements your body makes, including turning your shoulders and body at the waist. After a while, it will become a familiar set of movements.

Remember that your head stays still as your left shoulder turns underneath your chin. Your left arm is drawn across your chest during the backswing.

Swing clinic

Be patient. It will take time and lots of practice to groove your swing so that it feels natural and you are able to repeat the same swing again and again. With so many tips and thoughts in your head, it is common to tense up at the start of the swing. Try instead to ease your grip and feel loose. You need to be relaxed for your swing to work at its best.

Remember, the aim of your address position, stance, and swing is to get the clubface hitting the ball cleanly and squarely. Focus on what it feels like when you hit a good shot. You should hardly have felt the impact of the club on the ball.

Keep the first part of your backswing—the takeaway—low to the ground.

Make sure you are gripping the club relatively lightly. Some players find that a shake of their shoulders and arms just before they address the ball with the club loosens them up a little.

Your follow-through should leave you upright and balanced. If you topple off your feet, your swing may be too fast and not under control or your stance could be too narrow or unbalanced.

Loss of control of club

Body leaning back

On your backswing, your wrists should not change position until the club is approximately parallel to the ground.

Your wrists hinge to point the clubhead upward toward the sky during your backswing.

1 Keep your knees flexed a little throughout your swing, but only by a small amount so that you do not reduce your height at all.

2 Take the club away from the ball slowly and smoothly on your backswing. The club should rise vertically as your arms pass parallel to the ground.

3 With your hands leading your club on the downswing, your wrists should still be just ahead of the clubhead as it strikes your golf ball.

4 Don't lean back or rise up as you follow through. Keep your head still and think about your weight transfer through the shot.

FLEXING: the gentle bending of the knees in a golf swing

Golf terms

Swing faults

Learning to identify mistakes and correcting them is a crucial part of your golf education. Many swing faults occur as the result of poor grip, stance, or alignment when you address the ball. Others, such as topping—when you clip the top of the ball—may be caused by mistakes during your swing such as not keeping your head down or letting your legs straighten as you swing.

Standing too far away from the ball can lead to toeing—hitting the ball with the toe end of your club. Another cause is your arms tensing up during the swing and pulling the clubhead toward your body.

Keeping your chin down restricts the swing

X

Give yourself space to swing past your body

✔

An "L" shape aids speed and strength

X

✔

Try to create space for your arms and body to move in your set-up position. Standing too close to the ball can disrupt your swing and lead to your shanking the ball—hitting the ball with the part of the clubhead that joins the shaft.

Creating an "L" shape during the backswing helps increase clubhead speed and enables the club to approach the ball at a good angle, leading to a solid strike. If you do not hinge your wrists and instead keep them as straight as your arms, you are more likely to hit the ground before the ball, top the ball, or get less distance on your shot.

This golfer (on the far left) has not lined up his shot correctly, and as a result, he is leaning back, with his clubface open, just before connecting with the ball. This is likely to send the ball far to the right of his target. Try to make sure your clubface is square when it connects with the ball.

If you grip too far to the left or turn your shoulders too early, or if the ball is too forward in your stance, you may hit the ball with an open clubface. This can cause a slice— the ball starts left but swerves right of target.

Get a golf teacher to watch your swing and help you figure out flaws.

Arms extend ahead

A common mistake is to hinge the wrists and bend the elbows during the follow-through to send the clubhead upward too early. Your arms should extend during your follow-through.

Your weight should mostly be over your back foot at the top of your backswing. Too much weight over your front foot at this point means that you may chop down into the ground, causing weak, badly struck golf shots.

Try to keep your left arm relatively straight. Bending it too much at the elbow will reduce the swing speed and will leave no room for the club to swing down to the ball at the correct angle.

FOLLOW-THROUGH: the part of the swing after the ball has been hit by the club

Golf terms

Putting from different distances will help you learn to adjust the length of your putting swing.

Practice

Frequent practice is the only way to improve your game. Practice can be fun, varied, and challenging, though. You can practice your stance and grip at home and your putting with a cup as a target. You can practice swings without a ball in your backyard (with a piece of carpet to protect the grass) or by using a training ball attached to a short rod or cord.

Don't practice aimlessly. Always set targets and concentrate as you would if you were on a real golf course. Practicing hard between a series of golf lessons is a great way to improve because you can put into practice the tips and exercises that you learned in your previous lesson.

A small adjustment to your grip or positioning can lead to major improvements in accuracy.

A golf teacher, or pro, adjusts a young player's hand position as she addresses a putt. A good golf teacher can answer questions, improve your technique, and give you goals to aim for.

Head is directly
over the ball

Many golf courses have a practice
hole. This is ideal for practicing
and improving your bunker shots.

A small chipping net provides a
simple target to aim short chip
shots into at a park or in your yard.

Golfer checks
grip is correct
before putting

Many golf schools use high-speed video cameras to
record a golfer's swing. The videos can be replayed in
slow motion, paused, and zoomed into as a teacher
highlights areas where improvements can be made.
Your swing can even be compared to a top pro's.

This golfer is checking
his alignment and putting
stroke using two clubs to
form a corridor, through
which he will putt the
ball. The clubs give him
a strong visual aid to see
if his putting swing is
accurate or not.

Masterclass

Clubface is
square to ball

Vijay Singh
Top pros practice hard,
and few harder than Fiji's
Vijay Singh, who often hits
hundreds of balls during
a day's practice. Singh
hits groups of balls with
each club, working on one
type of shot at a time.

Woods laid on
the green form
a corridor

ALIGNMENT: how a golfer lines up their club and body relative to the ball and the target they are aiming for

Golf terms

Teeing off

Your first shot off the tee sets you up for the rest of the hole. When playing with others, the player who scored the lowest score on the previous hole has honors, meaning that they tee off first. Tee up your ball between the two tee markers and up to two club lengths behind. Plan where you want to send the ball to leave you with the best possible next shot.

A good tee height allows you to see at least the top half of the ball above a wood's clubhead when you address the ball.

You need a good, balanced stance with your feet placed a little wider apart than your shoulders. If using a long club such as a driver, stand a little farther away from the ball. Although it is tempting to swing harder and faster, try to complete a smooth, full swing that sweeps the ball off the tee.

Hold the ball and tee between your fingers and push the tee into the ground.

The club is taken away on a wide, full backswing. The right knee is kept slightly bent to help control the club.

The club swings down smoothly and with good rhythm. Don't lunge or push the club down with your hands.

Keep your eyes focused on the back of the ball as the clubhead sweeps through the ball smoothly.

Your body continues to turn as you follow through, with your back foot turning to finish on its toe.

When using a driver, set up so that the ball is in line with the heel of your front foot.

After following through, watch your ball in flight to pinpoint its location. Replace any divot.

Know how far you can hit the ball to decide whether to lay up short or try to clear bunkers across the fairway.

This hole doglegs to the left, so aim down the right-hand side of the fairway for the best possible second shot.

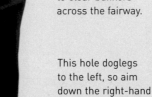

When there are hazards along the left to avoid, tee up on the left-hand side of the teeing area and aim away from them.

Knees are slightly flexed

Wide stance for balance

Golf terms | **LAY UP**: a decision made by a golfer to play a shorter than maximum-length shot to avoid a hazard

Fairway play

Although some players prefer to use a 3- or 4-wood or a hybrid club to play off a level part of the fairway, most fairway shots use irons. As with your drive, plan your shot, knowing how far you can hit the ball with a certain club, and aim where you want the shot to land—don't just hit the ball up the fairway aimlessly.

A hybrid, or rescue club, is a modern innovation. It is a cross between a wood and an iron and offers good control on the fairway Many players find such clubs easier to use than long irons such as a 2- or 3-iron.

1 On an uphill slope, lean into the slope and get more of your body weight over your front foot to stop you from falling back.

2 If the slope is steep, it will send the ball upward, so use one club longer than usual (a 5-iron instead of a 6-iron, for example).

Line up the ball between your feet. With longer irons, the ball should be closer to your front foot in the stance. With medium irons, it should be more in the center of your stance. Even if your ball is on the smooth, short grass of a fairway, you may be left with a tricky shot. Many fairways aren't perfectly flat, which can leave you playing a shot from a downward, upward, or sideways slope.

A good iron shot is likely to see a clump of turf fly away as you strike the ground. This is called a divot and should be replaced to help take care of the course.

This fairway shot with a lofted iron sends a large divot of turf flying away.

Collect the pieces of grass and press them gently back in place. Don't stamp down, as you might damage the roots.

Remember, you have to play your ball as it lies if it rolls into an unreplaced divot hole.

When playing a shot aiming for the green, think about where you expect the ball to bounce and roll and allow for wind or for a strong slope on the fairway or the green.

1 With the ball below your feet, bend your knees more, keep your weight a little on your toes, and lean into the slope.

2 The ball will tend to fly left to right, so aim a little left of your target. If it's a severe slope, use a three-quarter swing for more control.

Fairway shots aimed at the green are called approach shots. When playing an approach shot, choose your club carefully to send the ball the correct distance. Check carefully for the bunkers and other hazards lurking around the green.

DIVOT: a piece of turf torn out of the ground by a shot that must always be replaced

Golf terms

Pitch shots

A pitch shot is a high-flying, relatively short shot made usually with a 9-iron, pitching wedge, or sand wedge. The ball travels high and, if hit well, generates backspin, which means that the ball will stop relatively quickly after it lands and may even roll back. Pitch shots are used to land the ball on the green but also to clear obstructions such as a bush or to get back onto a fairway.

Pitch shots are made with a shortened version of your full swing. You can vary the distance of a pitch both by your club choice and how far you take the club back on the backswing. Gauging the distance to your target and what sort of pitch to play comes only with practice and experience.

At the point of contact, the clubface hits the ball squarely. The loft of the clubface sends the ball up high so you don't need to lean back or scoop the shot.

Seen from above, this golfer is playing a short pitch shot with an open stance. Her feet point to the left of the target.

Ball is far back in the stance

1 To play a regular pitch shot, set up with the ball in the center of your stance with a fraction more weight over your back foot.

Avoid scooping up the ball by keeping your head down as long as you can during your follow-through.

Keep an even speed throughout the pitch shot. A smooth, even tempo on the backswing, downswing, and follow-through is far more likely to result in a well-struck shot.

Think shorter backswing, good rhythm, and long follow-through for accurate pitch shots.

2 Turn your shoulders on the backswing, but aim for your hands to reach about shoulder height for a three-quarter swing, or lower if you plan a shorter shot. Let your wrists hinge fully to give a good "L" shape.

3 Swing normally on the way down, keep your head down as long as possible, and let the club follow through naturally high.

Practice your pitching often to learn how far to take the club back to generate different distances. Set up targets at different distances to aim for.

Practice pitching by playing ten shots with your hands taken back to just above waist height, then chest height, and shoulder height. Note how far the ball carries in the air, where it lands, and how far it rolls on. Repeat with different pitching clubs.

BACKSPIN: the spin on the ball that sees it stop quickly after landing

Golf terms

Chipping

Chip shots are relatively short, low-flying shots mostly used to get the ball close to the flag from a point off the green. Chips are also sometimes used to play the ball low out of a difficult situation, such as avoiding the overhanging low branches of a tree. Chipping involves a different stance and swing than other shots. This can feel strange at first, but persevere because it can be a very accurate stroke —it can get the ball close enough to the flag for you to complete the hole with a single putt.

PRO TIPS

Practice chipping with different clubs, from the 6-iron up to the pitching wedge, to see how each carries the ball differently.

The chip shot swing is short and is played with firm wrists throughout. Top players plan their shot just like they would a putt and pick a target point, usually just on the green, to aim the ball to land on with its first bounce. If they pick the right spot and execute the shot well, they expect the ball to roll up and down the contours of the green to get very close to the hole.

Wrists bend a little naturally as the club is taken back during a chip, but they don't hinge like they would in a pitch shot.

Avoid leaning back as you chip to try to lift the ball. Keep your weight on your front side.

Don't let your wrists cock in an attempt to scoop up the ball—keep them firm during the shot.

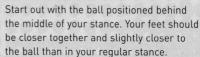

1 Start out with the ball positioned behind the middle of your stance. Your feet should be closer together and slightly closer to the ball than in your regular stance.

Avoid scooping up the ball in your shot.

Chip shots rely on your doing your homework first. Check the slopes and speed of the green and try to figure out the line that you want the ball rolling along.

Grip farther down the club to give you more control

Weight more on your left-hand side

Club brushes grass on the way through the ball

 The club is taken back smoothly and under control. Even the longest chip should not see the club reach the horizontal position on the backswing.

 Your hands lead the clubhead through the shot, with your arms staying ahead of the clubhead before and during impact.

 Keep your head down and wrists firm as the club follows through. The clubhead should end pointing toward the target rather than up and over your shoulder.

IMPACT: the point in a swing when the club makes contact with the ball

Golf terms

Bunkered!

Bunkers lie in wait on the fairway and around the green for shots that aren't hit with perfect accuracy. Don't be dismayed if you watch your ball land in or roll into the bunker—good bunker play, mostly using a sand wedge or another lofted club, can save you many dropped shots. With all bunker shots, make sure that your club doesn't touch the sand at address, or two penalty strokes will be added to your score.

If your ball lands directly in a bunker, it can rest deep in the sand. You'll need to hit powerfully behind the ball with your sand wedge.

The splash shot is the most common way of getting the ball out of a bunker. With an open stance and your club hovering just above the sand, swing your club smoothly back and then down. Your clubhead should lag just behind your hands as the shot is made. Keep your eyes on the spot in the sand where you want the club to strike the sand—about 1–2 in. (3–6cm) behind the ball. Don't let your club's swing die in the sand. Instead, follow through smoothly, with your upper body turning to face the target.

When you address the ball, wriggle your feet a little to get a good grip in the sand. Hover the clubhead above the sand and behind the ball.

Tiger Woods plays a bunker splash shot, hitting through the sand behind the ball, which lifts the ball into the air. His feet and legs are in an open stance, pointing to the left of his target.

Don't speed up your swing to force the ball out of the sand.

Always enter and leave a bunker from its most shallow side, so you don't damage the steep bunker face.

Always rake the sand smooth after playing a bunker shot to leave it in perfect condition for other golfers.

The entire shot should be smooth and have good rhythm. Your club should follow through about the same distance as the length of the backswing.

Masterclass

Sergio Garcia

Top bunker players, such as Spain's Sergio Garcia, trust the heavy sole of their sand wedge to cut through the sand and lift the ball out of a bunker. Garcia always takes his time in bunkers, focusing on a spot ahead where he wants the ball to land before playing the shot.

OPEN STANCE: where a golfer's feet and, sometimes, shoulders point to the left of the target

Golf Terms

Rough luck

Landing in the rough or another tricky position is all part of golf. If you are in a tough lie and position, look for the shortest and easiest route to the fairway, even if that shot won't leave you much closer to the hole. If your ball is sitting well in lighter rough, you can use your regular swing but with a hybrid or lofted club, such as a 7-iron, to get the ball out of trouble. Heavier rough may call for a different shot (see right).

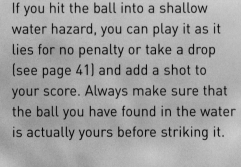

Tiger Woods completes his follow-through after using an iron to strike his ball from the light rough. Woods and other top pro golfers assess the precise lie of their ball to figure out what type of shot they can safely play.

Watch precisely where your ball lands in a water hazard in order to recover it.

If you hit the ball into a shallow water hazard, you can play it as it lies for no penalty or take a drop (see page 41) and add a shot to your score. Always make sure that the ball you have found in the water is actually yours before striking it.

A good lie in the rough means that you can play a regular medium- or short-iron shot.

Watch out for the rough's long grass grasping and twisting the clubhead.

1 To get out of heavy rough, use a lofted club such as a wedge and get more of your body weight over your front foot.

2 The ball is closer to your back foot than your front in the stance. Swing steeply downward with a little more speed than usual.

3 Keep the club moving through the grass as it hits down and through the back of the ball. The angle of the clubface should propel the ball upward.

4 Turn your hips as the shot is played and continue to turn as you perform a good, long follow-through.

You can move loose impediments (such as stones and twigs) and artificial obstructions (such as litter) away from your ball for no penalty. You are not, however, allowed to flatten down the grass or scrub. If you moved the grass away to find your ball, replace it without moving the ball.

PRO TIPS

Keep a firmer grip than usual on your club in long rough so the clubface is not twisted by the grass.

If your lie is good, you can sometimes punch a shot low below the branches of a tree. Address with your hands ahead of the ball and use a three-quarter swing of a medium iron with a shortened follow-through.

To judge the effect of the grass on your club, always take practice swings in rough, far away from your ball.

HYBRID: a club that is a cross between a wood and an iron

Golf terms

A ball in deep rough has to be played where it lies. Your one alternative is to decide that it is unplayable, drop the ball, and add a shot to your score.

Lost

Bad shots happen. They can lead to your losing your ball or finding it in a difficult position. If your ball is lost, you add a shot to your score and play a new ball from as close as possible to your lost ball's starting position. If you lose a ball off the tee, you can return to the tee, where your next shot will count as your third.

Your ball may come to rest against a loose twig or an artificial obstruction such as a soft drink can or other piece of litter. These items can be moved, provided you do not move the ball.

Ernie Els looks for his ball during the 2004 British Open. You can search for up to five minutes. After that, your ball is considered lost and you must play another ball, with a penalty shot and the original shot added to your score.

This player fears his ball (blue) is lost, so he plays a second, provisional ball (red). If his first ball is found, he must play it. If not, he plays the second ball, adding on a penalty shot and the original shot to his score.

If you want to drop your ball, take the longest club out of your bag—this is usually the driver.

Use the club to measure two club lengths away from the ball's original position, but not closer to the hole.

From that position, stand up straight and drop the ball from shoulder height with your arm stretched out fully.

If your ball is in an unplayable lie, you can replay the shot from its starting point or take a drop, but in both cases you have to add a penalty shot to your score. A dropped ball has to be redropped if it rolls out of bounds, into a hazard, onto the green, or more than two club lengths away from the original position.

Out of bounds on a golf course is usually shown by white markers. A ball hit out of bounds cannot be played and the shot must be replayed from the original position.

PRO TIPS

If searching for a ball with golfers waiting behind, wave them through so that they can continue playing.

PROVISIONAL BALL: a second ball hit from the same spot as the last shot when the first ball may be lost or out of bounds

Golf terms

On the green

Putting is where you will save the most shots if playing well—or rack up a big score if you putt poorly. Good putting sees the ball struck smoothly and cleanly so that the ball rolls along the green without jumping or bobbling. Your wrists and hands stay in the same position and do not hinge during a putt. Instead, the club, shoulders, and arms move together as a single unit, just like a pendulum.

Head stays rock steady throughout putt

Left shoulder stays down on the backswing

Elbows bent and tucked in

Hands grip lightly with both thumbs pointing down the club shaft

Clubface perfectly square to ball and just behind it

Ball closer to front foot in the stance

Stillness is key to accurate putting. Your head should stay down and remain perfectly still until long after the putt has left your club. From the waist down, nothing should move, either. Your body weight should be spread evenly between both feet. Your putter should travel in an arc from backswing to follow-through. The putter face stays square to the ball, while your feet point along a line parallel to the line the ball will travel.

Focus on the back of the ball and stay still. Make sure you don't nudge the ball at address, or that will count as a shot.

You can choose to putt even when you are not on the green. If your ball is on the green's apron or has a good lie, and the grass is short ahead, a putt can be a more accurate shot for a beginner than a short chip or pitch.

Keep your hands level with or ahead of the ball during the stroke.

Your shoulders start the putting movement as the putter is brought back slowly. Try to swing the putter head back and forward at the same speed, with the clubhead staying low to the ground. Your head remains still, and the "Y" shape formed by your arms and club doesn't alter as the club strikes the ball and follows through, with its face pointing in the direction of the ball's path.

Greens are rarely perfectly flat, so you have to line up where you are going to send the ball to allow for slopes. For more on reading the green, turn the page.

To improve your aim during practice, line up the ball on the green with the ball's logo pointing along the line in which you want to hit the ball.

This golf pro is holding a club vertically to check that the player's head is directly over the ball.

APRON: the closely mown area surrounding the green

Golf terms

This player is allowing for a left-to-right slope by aiming his ball to a point left of the hole (blue line). The ball will head toward that point before breaking and curving down and right toward the hole.

Line up your putter head behind the ball in the precise direction you want to stroke the ball. Then line up your feet and body around the club and ball.

This player is reading the green, assessing how much it slopes in order to figure out the best line for her putt.

In the hole

Practice your putting. Your stroke needs to be rock solid and repeatable with great accuracy under pressure. On many greens, you face the challenge of learning to understand the slopes and contours in order to know the precise line to send your ball on so that it will roll toward, and hopefully into, the hole. You must also learn to figure out the amount of force you need to send the ball the correct distance.

Gently lift dented grass with a ball mark repair tool. Finish by pressing down gently with the sole of your putter.

To read a green, crouch down some distance behind your ball and let your putter hang down vertically. You should be able to see how the green slopes. A slope will take a ball on a curving path, and you have to plot a target point to aim the ball at to allow for the slope.

To remove your ball out of the way or to clean it, place a marker behind the ball without nudging it and then lift it away.

As you walk around a green checking out the slopes, be careful not to step on the line of another golfer's putt.

Always putt straight at your target point and let the slopes do their work.

Line needed to allow for slope

Straight line to hole

Masterclass

To hit longer putts, don't swing faster or force the club forward. Instead, lengthen your backswing and swing smoothly and at the same speed to increase the distance your ball travels. Try to putt with enough force that if your ball misses the hole, it travels 12–24 in. (30–60cm) past it. Many beginners are too tentative and leave their putts yards short of the hole.

Padraig Harrington
Padraig Harrington takes time to read a green before he lines up his putt. The Irishman is known as an accurate putter, which has helped him win three Majors and many other tournaments. On the PGA tour he is often one of the players to take the fewest putts per round.

Remember key rules on the green, including placing the flagpole down gently. You are not allowed to take practice putts with a ball, but you can pick up any loose impediments such as a leaf or twig in the way of your putt.

LINE: the expected path of the ball to the hole

Golf terms

Getting around

Plotting a low-scoring way around golf holes is called course management. Knowing how far you can hit the ball with different clubs will help you plan and take fewer shots, as will understanding course conditions. For example, when the course is wet, your ball will roll far less than when it is dry and hard. Bad shots and decisions happen, but put them out of your mind and concentrate on how to get out of trouble safely.

Jack Nicklaus
Jack Nicklaus was able to plot his way around a course in as few shots as possible time and time again. This helped him avoid many bad rounds, stay in contention, and win 114 professional tournaments.

Use the time walking between shots to focus on the hole and how best to complete it.

- experienced junior
- excellent adult amateur
- newer player

Teeing area

Three golfers attempt this hole. Blue knows that he can drive long and clears the stream. Red's drives are shorter, so he lays up before the stream. Yellow is a newer player and hits a short drive.

Check wind strength and direction by throwing some loose grass into the air. If the wind is strong, you may want to change your club.

If your putt is on the same line as that of another golfer, watch theirs carefully. This is called "going to school."

Missing a short putt is annoying, but put it out of your mind and focus on making the next putt.

par 4

Blue aims straight for the green. Both blue and red want to get their ball onto the green's top level for an easier putt.

Red's second shot is down the left of the fairway, leaving a good angle to the flag.

After a short drive, yellow plays his second shot short of the stream. He then hits a long shot, but it lands in the steep face of the bunker. Rather than risk more trouble by aiming forward, he hits out sideways and then chips the ball onto the green.

Your lie in a fairway bunker determines what shot you can play. Here, the player has a good lie and, instead of a wedge, can play a 7-iron to reach the green.

LIE: where a player finds their golf ball has come to rest

Numbers game

Golf games are scored in different ways. When playing for fun, you simply record the shots you take and try to take as few as possible. Stroke play competitions are similar, and the winner is the golfer who takes the fewest shots of all. In match play, golfers play an opponent directly over a number of holes and win a hole by taking fewer strokes than their rival to complete it. If both players take the same number of shots, then a hole is halved.

A golf pro explains a rule to young players. If you want to play in competitions, getting a rulebook and learning all of the sport's rules is essential.

When playing against others, golfers mark their ball with a pen so that they can identify it at all times. Playing the wrong ball results in penalties.

Hole number

Stroke index ranks a course's holes from 1 to 18, with 1 being the hardest hole

Yardage from men's tees

1	TEE	
X	WHITE	72
	YELLOW	72
	RED	74

HOLE	YARDS	PAR	YA
1	524	5	
2	365	4	
3	426	4	
4	195	3	
5	444	4	43
6	391	4	37
7	137	3	135
8	548	5	536
9	413	4	398
3443	36	3320	
10	317	4	300
11	500	5	485
12	414	4	399
13	139	3	130
14	381	4	360
15	403	4	386
16	346	4	341
17	165	3	160
18	362	4	360
3027	35	2921	35
3443	36	3320	36
6470	71	6241	70

MARKER'S SIGNATURE

The Royal and Ancient Golf Club of Saint Andrews in Scotland is thought of as the home of golf. A separate organization, the R&A, rules on golf all over the world except in the United States and Mexico, where golf is governed by the United States Golf Association.

GOLF COMPETITION

ly 10

			Buckley		H/CAP	STROKES RECEIVED
					21	

PTS.	B	PTS.	YARDS	PAR	STROKE INDEX
			461	5	13
			336	4	5
			426	5	3
			165	3	15
			358	4	11
			361	4	1
			137	3	17
			450	5	9
			383	5	7
			3077	38	
			259	4	10
			468	5	6
			379	4	4
			115	3	18
			350	4	2
			376	5	12
			312	4	16
			140	3	14
			337	4	8
			2736	36	
			3077	38	
			5813	74	

PLAYER'S SIGNATURE M. Buckley

Player's score

Yardage from junior tees

Total yards for front nine holes

Total yards for back nine holes

In pro tournaments, referees on the course give rulings on difficult matters such as whether a ball is unplayable or not.

Scores over par are shown on a scoreboard with a plus sign. Above, Stefan Langer's 49 over par score is displayed after two rounds of the 2007 KLM Open tournament.

When you play regularly at a course, you can obtain a handicap. This is a number of shots that allow you to compete equally with a better golfer. Junior golfers can have a handicap of up to 36. Pro golfers play off zero. In a stroke play competition, your handicap is taken off the shots you take in order to give your final score.

A typical golf scorecard can look complicated, but it is actually easy to fill in. Make sure you write your scores in accurately or you will be disqualified from a tournament.

Golf is a polite, respectful sport. Win or lose, you should always shake hands with an opponent at the end of a game.

STROKE INDEX: the difficulty of a hole shown as a number from 1–18

Golf terms

What is a yard?
1 yard = 3 ft. (0.9m)
100 yards = 300 ft. (91m)
500 yards = 1,500 ft. (457m)

Professional golf

Top professional, or pro, golfers are paid to play and compete in dozens of different tournaments all over the world. With millions in prize money up for grabs, the competition is fierce. The very best golfers compete on the PGA Tour in the United States or the European Tour, while other regional tours such as the Japan Golf Tour and Asian Tour are also organized. Below these are satellite or challenge tours. Success on these tours may enable a young pro golfer to "earn his or her card" to join a bigger tour.

Top pros, such as Colin Montgomerie, maiɴ play as individuals in tournaments held over four rounds of 18 holes. They may also take part in team match play events, the most famous being the Ryder Cup for men and the Solheim Cup for women.

"You can always become better."
Tiger Woods

At the other end of their careers, veteran golfers can join seniors or champions tours. Eleven players, including Tom Watson, Hale Irwin, and Tom Kite, have already won more than $20 million on the PGA Champions Tour for players over 50 years of age.

Camilo Villegas's unusual putt-reading technique has earned him the nickname of "Spiderman." Like all pro golfers, the Colombian relies on input from his caddie.

Exciting young golfer Rory McIlroy entered the world top 20 as a teenager when he won the 2009 Dubai Desert Classic.

Sergio Garcia plays out of a bunker during the 2008 Ryder Cup. Each team had 12 players who contested a total of 28 matches. The U.S. team beat Garcia's European team 16.5 points to 11.5.

Fans dressed as Irish leprechauns cheer on the European team at the 2008 Ryder Cup. Thousands of spectators flock to major tournaments to watch top players in action.

CADDIE: a person who carries a golfer's clubs and offers advice

The Majors

The biggest professional tournaments of all are known as the Majors. There are four Majors for men's golf and four for women's golf. The men's calendar begins with the Masters, then the British Open (also known as the Open Championship), the U.S. Open, and finally the PGA Championship. The British Open was first held in 1860, making it the oldest of all the Majors and the only one of the four not held in the United States. The four women's Majors are the Kraft Nabisco Championship, the LPGA Championship, the U.S. Open, and the British Open.

Inbee Park (above) celebrates with fellow Korean golfer Ji Young Oh after Park won the 2008 U.S. Women's Open by four shots. She was just 19 years old at the time.

The 2009 Masters champion, Angel Cabrera, receives the famous green jacket from the previous year's winner, Trevor Immelman.

Y. E. Yang celebrates as his birdie on the 18th at Hazeltine saw him beat Tiger Woods to become the winner of the 2009 PGA Championship. Yang became the first Major winner born in Asia.

"If there's a golf course in heaven, I hope it's like Augusta National."

Gary Player

Brittany Lincicome tees off at the 5th hole at the 2009 Kraft Nabisco Championship. She won the tournament in dramatic fashion with an eagle on the very last hole and celebrated by jumping into a nearby lake.

"Any golfer worth his salt has to cross the sea and try to win the British Open."

Jack Nicklaus

Jean van de Velde stands in the water as his hope of winning the 1999 British Open starts to fade. He led the eventual winner, Paul Lawrie, by ten shots at the start of the fourth round.

Kenny Perry reacts after missing a putt during the 2009 Masters. Perry was almost the oldest Masters' winner, at 49, but lost in a play-off to Argentina's Angel Cabrera.

Padraig Harrington celebrates winning the 2008 British Open by three shots. Harrington won the tournament the previous year, a feat that Tiger Woods, Lee Trevino, and Tom Watson have also achieved.

The prestige of winning a Major, along with high prize money (in 2009, the men's PGA, Masters, and U.S. Open all offered $1.35 million to the winner), attract the world's very best golfers. This tends to lead to memorable and intense competition. From 2006 to 2009, for instance, the 16 women's Majors saw 15 different winners.

PLAY-OFF: a competition to determine the winner if the lowest scores are tied

Golf terms

The Saint Andrews Old Course started out with 22 holes, but in 1764 this was reduced to 18, becoming the world standard.

Great holes

There are thousands of golf courses around the globe. Some of them are world famous for their location and design, as well as because they host major competitions, from Solheim and Ryder Cup team golf tournaments to the men's and women's Majors. A number of courses have signature holes that are among the most photographed and most famous holes in golf.

The Old Course at Saint Andrews, Scotland, is one of the oldest and most famous in golf. Bleak and treeless in places, some holes share giant greens—meaning that you can reach the putting surface but still be more than 65 yd. (60m) away from the hole. The Old Course has hosted the British Open 28 times, most recently in 2010.

Teeing area for the 17th—the Road Hole

Old Course Hotel (with toughened glass windows)

David Duval took four shots to get out of the Road Hole bunker at the 2000 British Open, one less than Tommy Nakajima took at the 1978 Open.

The 17th hole at the Old Course is a par-four dogleg with the tee set right up against an out-of-bounds wall. The fairway is very narrow in places, the rough is treacherous, and there is the deadly deep Road Hole bunker (right) in front of the green to avoid.

Cypress Point's first six holes are set in woodland, the next seven holes set in sand dunes, and the final five holes right on the coast.

Pacific Ocean

16th hole—231 yards

Designed by famous course creator Alister MacKenzie (who also designed Augusta National), Cypress Point in California is regularly voted one of the most outstanding golf courses in the world. Its long, par-three 16th hole is both beautiful and an awesome test of nerve. Golfers have to drive over the Pacific Ocean to reach the green, surrounded by large bunkers, with the threat of the ocean and its strong sea breezes always present.

18th and 9th greens alongside each other

Tom Weiskopf finished second in the Masters four times. At the 1980 Masters, he took 13 strokes to complete the 12th hole.

The course at Augusta National Golf Club is one of the most beautiful courses in world golf and every year is home to the Masters, one of the four Majors for men.

At 155 yards, the 12th hole is the shortest at Augusta National, but it is a stern test of a golfer's accuracy and judgment. Swirling winds, difficult bunkers, and giant azalea bushes lie in wait for any player who misjudges which club to take. Many mis-hit shots land in Rae's Creek in front of the green.

Rae's Creek

DOGLEG: a golf hole that has a major turn in the fairway to the left or right

Golf terms

Golfing legends

The game of golf has produced some awesome players from all over the world. Here are profiles of some of the game's legends, as well as modern golf's rising stars.

Anthony Kim
A promising American talent, Kim has won on the PGA Tour and had an excellent Ryder Cup debut in 2008. He was part of the U.S. team that won the Presidents Cup in 2009.

Greg Norman
Australia's most successful pro golfer, Norman was an exciting, aggressive player who notched up more than 85 tournament victories in a long career. He missed out on many Majors, but he did win the British Open twice and was the world number one for 331 weeks.

Annika Sörenstam
Annika Sörenstam retired in 2008 at the age of 38, having won 90 tournaments, including ten Majors and more than $22 million in prize money. The first female golfer to score 59 in a competitive round, in 2005 Sörenstam became the first female golfer in almost 60 years to play in a male PGA tournament.

Bobby Jones
One of golf's first great champions was the amazing and unpredictable Bobby Jones. He played only as an amateur and retired at just 28, by which time he had already won the U.S. Open four times and the British Open three times. In 1930, he achieved the incredible feat of winning four Majors in the same calendar year.

Tom Watson

One of the United States' finest golfers, Watson has won 66 tournaments, including eight Majors. At age 59, Watson had a putt to win his sixth British Open in 2009 but went on to lose.

Ernie Els

Els first found fame in 1984, winning a Junior World Golf Championship title. He turned professional in 1989 and charmed spectators with his effortless swing, long-distance driving, and, at times, superb putting. Els has won 60 professional tournaments and has been ranked among the top-ten golfers in the world for more than 14 years.

Babe Zaharias

Babe Zaharias excelled at baseball, basketball, and track and field (winning an Olympic gold medal) before turning to golf. She had an enormous impact, winning ten Majors and, in 1946, an amazing 13 tournaments in a row. She helped found the Ladies' Professional Golf Association (LPGA) in 1949.

Michelle Wie

Wie (left) qualified for the USGA Amateur Championship at age ten and turned professional at 15. She has played 14 tournaments against men and has finished second or tied for third in all four women's Majors. In 2009, she achieved her first LPGA tournament win.

PGA: short for Professional Golfers' Association, the body that runs professional men's golf in the United States

Golf terms

Lorena Ochoa

Mexico's most successful golfer, Ochoa has won 27 LPGA tournaments in just five years, helped by her long driving and excellent putting under pressure. She was world number one from 2007 until her retirement in 2010.

Jack Nicklaus

The "Golden Bear" is thought of, by many, as the greatest pro golfer of all. He won his first Major in 1962 and his last in 1986, a total of 18, which remains a record. A superb competitor and thinker about the game, Nicklaus won more than 100 other competitions, while his golf course design company is now one of the largest in the world.

Phil Mickelson

Mickelson is the most successful left-handed player currently on the PGA Tour. His attacking play has seen him lose tournaments (he has come in second or tied for second in the U.S. Open five times) but win many fans. He has won four Majors as well as 33 other PGA Tour victories.

Tiger Woods

Woods has revolutionized men's professional golf, notching up 14 Majors and 95 tournament wins. He has been world number one for more than 570 weeks—an amazing 11 years. A serious knee injury disrupted his 2008–2009 seasons, but he still managed to win five tournaments in 2009 and finish second in the PGA Championship.

Ryo Ishikawa

Already a superstar in Japan, Ishikawa is still in his teens but has won six times on the competitive Japan Golf Tour. His first victory was at the age of 15, and in 2009, aged 18, he broke into the world top-50 ranked golfers.

Vijay Singh

Vijay Singh is the Pacific region's most successful golfer. A former world number one, Singh has won 58 professional tournaments, the Masters in 2000, and the PGA Championship twice.

Severiano Ballesteros

There were few more exciting sights in golf than Ballesteros in full flow. Sometimes wayward but blessed with great recovery shots, the Spaniard captured five Majors (between 1979 and 1988) and more than 50 European tournaments. An ardent enthusiast for the Ryder Cup, he has won five times as player and captain. He is best known for his great short game.

Sergio Garcia

Sergio Garcia is an attacking golfer who has won on the PGA and European tours and has already appeared in five Ryder Cups. He has finished fourth or better in all four Majors without winning one, but in 2008 he won more than $6.9 million, more than any other golfer.

Colin Montgomerie

Montgomerie dominated European golf in the 1990s, topping the annual earnings list on the PGA European Tour seven times in a row between 1993 and 1999 and again in 2005. The tall Scot, one of the greatest of all Ryder Cup players, has won 40 professional tournaments.

RECOVERY SHOT: a shot played out of difficulty such as from heavy rough

Golf terms

Extreme golf

Golf has conjured up many crazy moments. Players have struck strange shots or fallen foul of the weather or nearby wild animals. Golf legend Sam Snead was once chased by an on-course ostrich, while Gary Player and Jack Nicklaus left a hole early when they were attacked by bees. Not all animal encounters are negative, though. In 1981, amateur golfer Ted Barnhouse scored a hole in one after his drive bounced off a cow's head!

A golfer plays in the middle of London, England, during the 2006 Jameson Urban Golf event. Urban golf uses beanbag balls to prevent damage and a portable piece of turf from which to hit the ball.

The Africa-shaped green of the Xtreme 19th hole at South Africa's Legends Course is an extraordinary sight. The hole is a par three, but the tee is reached by helicopter, as it's a staggering 1,410 ft. (430m) above the green. A cool $1 million greets any golfer who scores a hole in one.

Courses can be crazy, too. The par-three 14th at the Coeur d'Alene course in Idaho has a floating green in a lake reached only by boat. Other courses are based in sandy deserts or in icy wastes, while urban golf games are sometimes played in cities.

Golf can even be played on snow, with the help of a colored ball. The World Ice Golf Championships are held in Greenland each year over nine snowy holes.

Masterclass

Bernhard Langer

At a 1981 tournament in Fulford, England, top pro golfer Bernhard Langer hit his approach shot on the 17th hole into the trees. The ball came to rest in the branches 16 ft. (5m) off the ground. Unfazed, Langer climbed up the tree and chipped the ball straight onto the green.

APPROACH SHOT: a stroke that sends the ball from the fairway onto or closer to the green

Golf terms

Glossary

addressing the ball
Taking your stance and getting ready to hit the ball.

alignment
How a golfer lines up their club and body relative to the ball and the target they are aiming for.

approach shot
A stroke that sends the ball from the fairway onto or closer to the green.

backswing
The movement of the club back and away from the ball.

ball marks
Dents in the green caused by a golf ball's landing.

birdie
Scoring one under par on a hole.

bogey
Scoring one over par on a hole.

caddie
A person who carries a golfer's clubs and offers advice.

divot
A piece of turf torn out of the ground by a shot that must always be replaced.

dogleg
A golf hole that has a major turn in the fairway to the left or right.

double bogey
Two over par on a hole.

eagle
Two under par on a hole.

etiquette
Good behavior and consideration for other golfers and the course.

fairway
The closely mown area, usually from tee to green, down which golfers aim their ball.

fore!
Warning shouted when it appears that your ball may be flying toward other golfers.

ground under repair
Areas on a golf course marked by the greenskeepers as being regrown or prepared. If your ball lands in such an area, a free drop can be taken without any penalty shots being added to the score.

handicap
A system used in amateur golf to give players of different abilities a chance to compete equally.

hole in one
Hitting the ball straight into the hole from the tee.

honors
A tradition that means the player with the lowest score on the previous hole is the first to tee off on the next hole.

hook
A shot that curves sharply left of the target line for a right-handed golfer.

impact
The point in a swing when the club makes contact with the ball.

lay up
A decision made by a golfer to play a shorter than maximum-length shot to avoid a hazard such as a bunker in front of a green.

lie
Where a player finds their golf ball has come to rest. As a general rule, your ball must be played as it lies without being moved.

line
The expected path of the ball to the hole.

loft
The amount of angle on the club face. A 9-iron, for instance, has much more loft than a 3-iron.

Majors
Four tournaments for men and four tournaments for women that are thought of as the pinnacle of professional golf.

open stance
When a golfer's feet and, sometimes, shoulders point to the left of the target.

play-off
A competition over one or more holes to determine the winner if more than one golfer is tied for the lowest score.

provisional ball
A second or subsequent ball hit from the same spot as the last shot when the first ball may be lost or out of bounds.

putt
A shot usually made on the green or close to it, in which the ball is rolled along the ground using the putter.

recovery shot
A shot played out of difficulty, such as from heavy rough.

rough
The area, often flanking a fairway, where grass is much longer and harder to hit the ball out of.

round
The name given to playing all the holes on a golf course. In many professional golf tournaments, golfers play four rounds in total.

sand wedge
A very lofted iron with a chunky sole, designed to get the ball out of a sand bunker.

short game
Shots that take place on or near the green. Putting, chipping, pitching, and greenside bunker play are all aspects of the short game.

slice
A shot that spins or curves away far to the right of the target for a right-handed player.

stroke index
A number from one to 18 that represents how hard each hole is in comparison to the others on the course. One is the hardest hole on a course.

stroke play
A scoring format for a competition where the winner is the player who takes the fewest shots to complete the scheduled number of holes.

tee
A peg on which the ball is placed for the first shot on a hole.

teeing area
The marked-out area at the start of a hole from which a player makes their first shot, called the drive.

tee markers
The colored markers placed on the teeing area. Golfers must play their drive in line with the markers and up to two club lengths behind them.

water hazard
An area of water permanently on the course such as a pond or stream.

yardage
The distance from the tee to the flag on a golf course.

Websites

www.juniorlinks.com
This website for golf juniors is run by the United States Golf Association. It can direct you to golf programs in you area and contains plenty of tips and links to other useful websites.

www.playgolfamerica.com
This site helps you find courses that welcome kids and families and offers tips on finding golf instruction.

http://espn.go.com/golf/
A good place to go for all professional golf news, the ESPN golf webpages also include the top men and women's professional rankings as well as videos.

www.thefirsttee.org
This is the website of The First Tee, an initivative of the World Golf Foundation that encourages young people to develop good character and life skills through golf.

www.pgatour.com
The website of the U.S. PGA Tour is full of information on upcoming tournaments as well as statistics and records.

www.lpga.com
The official website of the Ladies' PGA Tour includes golf tips for female golfers as well as lots of news and information on tournaments and top pro players.

www.europeantour.com
The official website of the PGA European Tour boasts plenty of interviews, features, and news from tournaments.

Index

Picture credits

The Publisher would like to thank the following for permission to reproduce their material. Every care has been taken to trace copyright holders. However, if there have been unintentional omissions or failure to trace copyright holders, we apologize and will, if informed, endeavor to make corrections in any future edition.

t = top; b = bottom; c = center; l = left; r = right
Pages 6 Getty/Joao Padua; 7 Corbis/Christina Salvador; 10 Corbis/Louie Psihoyos; 13 Shutterstock/Danny E. Hooks; 14 Shutterstock/Robert Kyllo; 14 Shutterstock/Theodor Ostojic; 14 Shuttersock/cycreation; 15t Shutterstock/Brad Thompson; 15b Corbis/Michael Yamashita; 17 Getty/Central Press; 19 Shutterstock/Barry Salmons; 21 Phil Sheldon Golf Picture Library; 26 Shutterstock/Barry Salmons; 36 Corbis/Charles W. Luzier; 37 Shutterstock/Barry Salmons; 38l Shutterstock/rusty426; 38r Corbis/Shaun Best/Reuters; 40–41 Phil Sheldon Golf Picture Library; 45 Shutterstock/Sportsphotographer.eu; 47 Shutterstock/Barry Salmons; 50b Getty/Don Emmert; 50tr Shutterstock/Sportsphotographer.eu; 50br Corbis/Toby Melville; 51t Getty/Harry How; 51b Getty/Fred Vulch; 52tr Getty/Scott Halleran; 52bl Getty/Jamie Squire; 52br Getty/David Cannon; 53t Getty/Stephen Dunn; 53cl Phil Sheldon Golf Picture Library; 53c Getty/Don Emmert; 53cr Phil Sheldon Golf Picture Library; 53b Shutterstock/photogolfer; 54 Getty/David Cannon; 55t Phil Sheldon Golf Picture Library; 55b Corbis/Tony Roberts; 56l Shutterstock/photogolfer; 56r Shutterstock/photogolfer; 57t Shutterstock/Danny E Hooks; 57b Shutterstock/photogolfer; 58tl Shutterstock/photogolfer; 58tr Shutterstock/LouLou Photos; 58cr Shutterstock/LouLou Photos; 58b Shutterstock/photogolfer; 59ct Shutterstock/Sportsphotographer.eu; 59cl Shutterstock/photogolfer; 59b Shutterstock/Sportsphotographer.eu; 60–61 With the Kind Permission of The Legends Resort, South Africa; 60tr Phil Sheldon Golf Picture Library; 61tl Shutterstock/Pedro Jorge Henriques Monteiro; 61b Phil Sheldon Golf Picture Library.